The Best Ghost Tales of North Carolina

Including stories from winners of
the statewide "Ghost Watch" contest

Terrance Zepke

illustrated by Julie Rabun

Pineapple Press, Inc.
Sarasota, Florida

This book is dedicated to my father, who firmly believes he is the driving force behind every success I achieve. Seldom wrong and right again, Dad.

Acknowledgments

There are many people I wish to thank for making this book possible. To the archivists and librarians at Davidson College, New Hanover County Public Library, University of North Carolina at Asheville, Cumberland County Public Library, University of North Carolina at Chapel Hill, North Carolina State Archives, Rhine Research Center/Institute for Parapsychology, and Outer Banks History Center, I am very grateful for your time and attention. I'd also like to extend a special thanks to Dave Thompsky at Grove Park Inn, Catherine Frank at Chapel Hill Preservation Society, Jeremy Carter at Peppertree Resorts, Vance Brown, Ardell Tiller, Don Patterson at Greensboro News & Record, and everyone at Pineapple Press, especially Alba Aragón, whose diligence and copyediting were much needed and greatly appreciated.

Inquiries should be addressed to:
Pineapple Press, Inc.
P.O. Box 3889
Sarasota, Florida 34230

www.pineapplepress.com

Photos, unless otherwise indicated, are by Terrance Zepke

Library of Congress Cataloging-in-Publication Data

Zepke, Terrance
    Best ghost tales of North Carolina / Terrance Zepke.—1st ed.
        p. cm.
"Including stories from winners of the statewide 'Ghost watch' contest."
Includes index.
ISBN 1-56164-233-9 (alk. paper)
  1. Ghosts—North Carolina. 2. Haunted houses—North Carolina. I. Title.

BF1472.U6 Z45 2001
133.1'09756—dc21

                                        2001021363

First Edition
10 9 8 7 6 5 4 3 2 1

Design by Shé Sicks
Printed in the United States of America

of Contents

Introduction

What are ghosts? Guardian angels? Lingering spirits of loved ones? Balls of energy that manifest themselves in various forms? Or, is it all a trick of the mind, as proponents of psychokinesis would have us believe?

Ever since I can remember, I have loved reading and listening to ghost stories. They are so intriguing on the surface, I guess I never wanted to examine the issue too closely, just in case I stumbled across scientific justification of the origin of the Brown Mountain Lights or what actually happened with the mysterious ship, *Carroll A. Deering.*

When I wrote *Ghosts of the Carolina Coasts,* I did not probe into the subject of ghosts from an academic standpoint. I concentrated on relaying some wonderful stories that took place from North Carolina's Outer Banks to the Low Country of South Carolina. I was certain I would end up writing another book on the subject, focused exclusively on North Carolina's folklore.

I wanted this publication to be different from other regional ghost books, since in addition to the sixteen traditional ghost stories and seven chapters on haunted houses, I conducted a statewide "ghost watch" contest. I enlisted the help of bookstores and the media through press releases detailing my mission. From the many entries, I chose four and offer them here. Furthermore, I have addressed the issue of how to determine if a place is haunted and how to document it by adding a chapter on how to conduct a "ghost hunt."

Determining which stories were "the best ghost tales of North Carolina" was of course difficult and finally arbitrary. I knew I had to include some well-known stories, but I wanted to share some lesser-known tales as well. Additionally, the cumulative stories had to be a good representation of the entire state.

When I started working on this book, I decided it was high time to address the "ghost issue." Do ghosts really exist? If so, who or what are they? I discovered that this is a very complicated matter. Some experts err on the side of caution to lend some credibility to the subject. Other authorities on the topic seem to go to the extreme with their discussions of the supernatural, the other side, poltergeists, and phantoms. I decided to investigate the topic, and here is what I learned.

By dictionary definition, parapsychology is "the study of phenomena such as telepathy, clairvoyance, and psychokinesis that are not explainable by known natural laws." Duke University in Durham, North Carolina, used to be one of only four universities in the world that offered a degree program in parapsychology.

According to the Rhine Research Center (formerly part of Duke University),

> Parapsychology is the science that lies "beside" or "beyond" psychology—it studies those unique experiences and unknown capabilities of the human mind that suggest consciousness is capable of interacting with the physical world in ways not yet recognized by science, but not beyond science's ability to investigate.

> Extrasensory perception (ESP) is the ability to acquire information without using the known senses. In cases when another person is involved, it may be considered telepathy, or mind-to-mind communication. When it is knowledge of just a distant place or event, the term clairvoyance is often used. In practice, because it is difficult to distinguish among types of ESP, investigators generally refer to just ESP. When the information seems to apply to some future event, it is called precognition. Real-life experiences that appear to involve ESP are commonly termed psychic experiences.

> Less common is Psychokinesis (PK), which is the direct influence of the human mind on the environment. In rare cases, this may involve obvious movement of objects, but most contemporary research studies PK influences on atomic or electronic processes.

Introduction

The dictionary's primary definition of ghost is "the spirit or shade of a dead person, supposed to haunt living persons or former habitats; specter; phantom; wraith." A poltergeist is "a ghost that manifests itself by noises and rappings."

Many experts believe that people are more than flesh and bone. They are energy. When a person dies, that energy does not necessarily go away or dissipate, especially if the deceased was a vibrant and energetic individual when he or she was alive. This is why the study of electromagnetic energy is one important tool used in scientific investigations of ghosts.

Some think that ghosts are spirits who simply won't accept that they had to leave the world or don't know how to get to the next world. It's believed that most spirits are harmless, mischievous, even protectors of sorts.

Experts generally agree that ghosts are not interactive, but poltergeists are mischievous—moving objects around. Interestingly, paranormal investigators don't believe poltergeists are connected to the spiritual realm. Instead, they believe an adult or child in a stressful situation unknowingly moves objects and so begins the legend of a haunted house. The situation is real, but the participant doesn't realize his or her involvement.

But what about those who claim to have seen a ghost? The current trend of thought by experts is that sightings are a place memory. These place memories can be detected by psychically sensitive people. These are right-brain persons, considered to be tuned into place memories, which could help explain why some people see ghosts and others (in the same place at the same time) don't see or sense anything. Paranormal researchers are inclined to believe that paranormal activity is related to magnetic and electric fields, which could be generated by clocks, radios, stereos, and high-tension wires. Constant exposure to these fields can increase psychic sensitivity. It's commonly believed that specters can take different forms, such as orbs, mists, vortexes, silhouettes, shadows, clouds, and faceless bodies. Or they can appear as they did when they were alive.

There are professional ghost hunters and spirit investigators. Ghost hunters apply scientific techniques, including the use of equipment (which is discussed in the last section of this publication). Spirit investigators see what the rest of us can't. When determining if a spirit is present in a particular place, they search for changes in energy or density and whether they feel electricity.

This is accomplished by exploring the locale and touching objects found therein. Individuals or teams of spirit investigators are sometimes called in to help rid a place of spirits. There's only one way to do this, according to the experts. Ask. Ask very nicely. A spirit cannot be forced out. The only way is to ask it to please leave and hope it will do so. Surprisingly, spirit investigators say this technique has met with success more often than not.

After all my research, I found myself more confused about specters than when I started. Ultimately, I decided to just sit back and enjoy a good ghost tale, and to leave the analysis to "experts."

The Ghost Tales

Legend of the Gimghoul Castle

Chapel Hill

Peter Dromgoole came to the University of North Carolina at Chapel Hill in 1831, but the eighteen-year-old failed his admissions test. After an argument with the professor who administered the test, the irate young man almost left Chapel Hill in a fit of temper. The spoiled lad really wasn't interested in school, but he didn't want to go home and tell everyone he wasn't accepted at Carolina. Dromgoole stayed and hired a tutor, presumably to help him pass the entrance exam at a later date.

Scholastics took a backseat to Dromgoole's real passions: playing cards and chasing women. Legend has it that the playboy met his match when he encountered a young woman named Fanny. The two usually met at Piney Prospect, which is the highest point in Chapel Hill. Peter and Fanny had an arrangement that suited them, and the pair carried on until their happiness was ruined by a jealous rival. Another man became obsessed with Fanny and challenged Dromgoole to a pistol duel. Male pride forced Peter to accept even though his competitor's skills were superior.

Late one night, the two men squared off at Piney Prospect. An old slave noticed the men getting ready to duel and ran to tell Miss

Gimghoul Lodge
University of North Carolina

Gimghoul Castle is accesible only to its caretaker and members of the
Order of the Gimghouls, a secret society.

Courtesy of North Carolina Collection, University of North Carolina at Chapel Hill

Fanny. The frightened woman ran as fast as she could but Dromgoole had already been shot by the time she arrived. Sobbing uncontrollably, she had no choice but to cradle her lover in her arms as he died. Witnesses to the deadly confrontation did not want their participation revealed, and they agreed to keep secret what had transpired that night. The men quickly dug a shallow grave, put the body in it, and covered it with a large stone (which later became known as Dromgoole's Tomb).

For a while, Fanny continued to go to Piney Prospect every day, where she felt closer to Peter. She would sit in front of the rock under which he was buried, alternately weeping, talking to him, and lovingly touching the slab that served as his tombstone. Fanny was unable to eat or sleep. The heartbroken woman lost her will to live and died shortly after Peter Dromgoole did.

Many believe that the site of this tragedy, including the castle that was built nearby years later, is haunted. Legend has it that sobbing and wailing are still heard at times. Dromgoole's Tomb is stained red, and whenever it rains a liquid that looks like blood seeps out of it.

According to James Vickers' *Chapel Hill: An Illustrated History* (Barclay, 1985), Peter's uncle heard the story of the duel and traveled to Chapel Hill to investigate. However, Congressman George Dromgoole was unable to find evidence of foul play or discover the truth about his nephew's abrupt and mysterious disappearance. A letter written by Peter Dromgoole's roommate, John Buxton Williams, attempted to dispel speculation. In his letter, the man denied there had been any violent encounter. Williams stated that Dromgoole "had simply left on a public stage." Some dismissed this, believing that the affluent Virginian family had pressured Dromgoole's roommate to write the letter to save the family's reputation from scandal.

Bruce Cotton, a descendant of Peter Dromgoole, found three letters from Peter Dromgoole to his family at the Brunswick County, Virginia, homestead, and published them in the November 1924 issue of *Carolina Magazine*. These letters support the story that Dromgoole failed his admissions test and then hired a tutor. In April 1833, the youth wrote his last letter, disclosing he was depressed and telling his father he was going to Europe. After this communication, he was never heard from again. Cotton believes Dromgoole did not go to Europe. Instead, he thinks the young man joined the Army using his former roommate's name and then moved to Texas, where he died in a gunfight.

Dr. Kemp Plummer Battle, a former president of the University of North Carolina at Chapel Hill, wrote *History of the University of North Carolina*. In this publication Battle mentions the Dromgoole legend. He is of the belief that Peter Dromgoole left UNC–Chapel Hill and migrated to the Southwest, where he was subsequently killed in a bar fight, possibly over a woman or a card game.

Chapel Hill has two historic districts: the UNC–Chapel Hill campus and the Gimghoul District, where Piney Prospect and the magnificent castle are located. Originally called Hippol Castle, the building has been dubbed Dromgoole's Castle because of the legendary duel. It is also popularly known as Gimghoul Castle, since it has been the gothic meeting place for the Order of the Gimghouls for over seven decades. Not much is known about the castle or the secret society that owns it.

The idea of building such a structure on this site originally belonged to Edwin Wray Martin, a former University of North

---

Charles Baskerville Jr.
(April 16, 1896–November 20, 1994)

This renowned artist was born in Raleigh and lived in Chapel Hill during part of his childhood. His work is respected and admired around the world. Jacqueline Kennedy Onassis owned two of his works: a watercolor-and-pencil sketch, "Tiger," and a painting, "Guardians of the Portal of the Temple." They fetched $40,250 and $23,000, respectively, in her estate auction in 1996. The artist donated a wall painting, "George and the Dragon," to the secret Gimghoul society shortly after the castle was built (in honor of his father, who had been a member).

Carolina student. The strange young man liked to climb up to Piney Prospect and roam the dense forest area, envisioning a magical wonderland filled with merlins and goblins. He dubbed the woods "Glandon Forest" and dreamed of an imposing, medieval edifice in the midst of the forest where he and other like-minded men could meet. Edwin Martin founded a small fraternity in 1889 based on his beliefs and ideals. The Order of the Gimghouls started out with just five members, including Martin. Before realizing his dream, Martin died in 1895, but the fraternity lived on. Members made shrewd and aggressive land deals, starting with the purchase of ninety-five acres. Subsequently, they traded part of that land to the university, sold some acres, and developed forty acres into a neighborhood. Using money earned from these deals, the society built the fabulous Gimghoul Castle.

The $50,000 construction project began in 1926 and took four years to complete. The massive gothic structure required 1,300 tons of well-rounded stones. The work was done by a crew of French stonecutters who were brought from Valdese and spoke no English.

Very few non-members have been allowed inside the castle, but those who have gained access say it is spectacular. They report there is a large banquet room, tower room, kitchen, caretaker's apartment, and grand spiral staircase. Once upon a time, there was medieval armor in the banquet room, but it was stolen.

The Order of the Gimghouls have placed floodlights that illuminate the castle and grounds at night and have posted several "No Trespassing" signs to let curiosity seekers know that they are not wanted or tolerated. There is a live-in caretaker, and police are dispatched when intrusions take place. The society allegedly consists of notable alumni, as well as some students and professors. Membership is usually "by legacy" and men are inducted periodically in elaborate ceremonies.

The secret fraternity published a booklet about the Gimghoul legend in 1978. The legend tells of a figure in a heavy, dark, hooded robe who appears at Dromgoole's room in South Building and uses an extended arm to signal Peter Dromgoole to the hilltop. This sinister figure is supposedly the unknown assailant who killed Dromgoole during the pistol duel. The booklet also claims that the ghost of Dromgoole rises from his grave at midnight on the anniversary of his death.

The secret society also divulged its emblem and its symbolism in this booklet. It is a ghoul behind a broken pillar holding a cross in his left hand and a key in his right. The key opens the Dark Secret of the Gimghouls and the cross stands for the Dark Secret itself. As to what the Dark Secret is, I doubt that it will ever be disclosed to "outsiders."

Hermit of Fort Fisher

Fort Fisher

Robert Edward Harrell was born on February 2, 1893, and he was put into a county rest home in Shelby, North Carolina, in 1955. That might have been the end of the story, but it is just the beginning of this tale. Determined not to be confined, he ran away to Fort Fisher, where he lived until his death on June 4, 1972. It was five years after he left the care facility that his family finally learned of his whereabouts.

For seventeen years he lived in an old World War II bunker and was pretty much self-sufficient, subsisting on berries, fish, shrimp, oysters, and vegetables that he grew. When the weather was bad, the hermit relied on the kindness of others for food. Harrell made periodic trips into town to get provisions he was unable to grow or catch himself. He revealed these insights into his life during a rare interview with a staff member of the Center for Southern Folklore.

The recluse informed the interviewer that he did not eat many square meals as he was just too busy. Harrell told family and visitors to Fort Fisher that he had moved there to write a book. He claims he finished a 400-page manuscript entitled *A Tyrant in Every House* and sent it to his sister in Charlotte for safekeeping.

Robert Edward Harrell, a.k.a. "The Hermit of Fort Fisher," at the dedication ceremony of Fort Fisher State Historic Site Visitor Center, 1960.
Courtesy of the N.C. Division of Archives and History

The hermit also told the interviewer that he had a son and nine grandchildren in Cleveland, Ohio. He said his son came to visit once a year. (The son later moved to Chattanooga, Tennessee, but he is now deceased.)

The colorful coot said he loved people, especially the underdog, the handicapped, and the working man. Indeed, he was friendly to all who spoke to him during their visit to Fort Fisher. As word spread about the Hermit of Fort Fisher, he became something of a tourist attraction. Although he made his home in the bunker, which was closed off by loose two-by-fours placed haphazardly around the entrance, Harrell claimed he spent most nights outside at the marsh. Yet the hermit was found dead, spread eagle with a raincoat bunched around his neck and his legs all bloody, *inside* the bunker with the two-by-fours barricading the entrance. Shoe prints were found in the sand that could have belonged to someone who dragged Harrell's body back to the bunker. Authorities who investigated his death believed he had a

I found the videotaped interview between the Hermit and a staff member of the Center for Southern Folklore in a public library. Strangely, when I contacted the center to get some additional information, no one knew what I was talking about. Judy Peizer, who has been director of the center for a long time, told me that the center had never participated in the interview or video. She said the center exists for the preservation of oral storytelling and performance art and that none of its employees would have been involved in such a project, even on a freelance basis. The director was completely baffled when asked why the center was credited with the project, and since the interviewer remained off camera, there is no way of knowing who was responsible for making the video. But Ms. Peizer acknowledged that the producer and media specialist (who were listed with the center's address in the credits) were former employees.

heart attack but managed to crawl from the marsh back inside the bunker. But did Harrell put the two-by-fours in front of the bunker entrance before finally dying?

It doesn't seem plausible. Long-time acquaintances, such as Gail Welker, are not swallowing this far-fetched story. Since there was evidence of a struggle, she is of the opinion that he was killed for the money he kept on hand to buy supplies. Supposedly, the Hermit hid his money in old jars and buried them in the sand. For whatever reason, officials did not pursue this possibility. During the interview conducted by the Center for Southern Folklore, the hermit said he had been threatened, even beaten, while living on Fort Fisher.

So what did happen? Did local hoodlums accidentally beat up the old man so badly they killed him and then tried to conceal it? Did they cause him to have a heart attack and then leave him for dead? Did robbers murder him for his buried money? Did developers who wanted the squatter off the prime piece of real estate murder him? Did he die a natural death? Some say we'll never know because the State Bureau of Investigation and the local

Before retreating from society, the Hermit was a printer, a
street vendor who sold trinkets and jewelry, a machinist, a
farm worker, and a coal miner.

Sheriff's Department bungled the investigation. Critics say the
body should have been autopsied before it was buried. They claim
a sloppy and half-hearted investigation was conducted and that
those involved have been trying to conceal that fact.

What we do know is that Captain H.G. Grohman, chief of
detectives with the Sheriff's Department, got a call from the
Carolina Beach Police informing him that the Hermit was dead.
Grohman called Fred Pickler, the department's unofficial photographer, to come with him and take the crime scene photographs.
When the men arrived they found a track extended thirty feet
from the bunker doorway to the edge of the marsh. The captain
thought it looked like the Hermit had suffered a heart attack,
crawled back inside the bunker, and died. Pickler said it looked like
someone had dragged the body by the feet, which explained why
the coat was bunched up around the neck. He photographed the
body, the mysterious tracks, and tire marks from a four-wheel-drive
vehicle, which appeared to be fresh. One of the photos clearly
shows that two-by-fours were in front of the bunker entrance,
which makes it impossible to believe that the old man put them up
while he was having a heart attack. A plaster of the tire tracks was
also made. Deputies found $300 hidden in cans and jars.

The body was taken to the morgue at New Hanover Memorial
Hospital. Without performing an autopsy, the medical examiner
determined the cause of death to be "heart attack." Curtis Register,
the SBI special agent sent to investigate the death, reviewed the
evidence and came to the conclusion that the questionable tracks
were made by a body that was dragged. But the agent didn't feel
he had enough evidence to officially call it a murder. The case was
closed six months later for lack of evidence.

Beth Purvis Farmer revealed that when she was a teenager, she
and a couple of her friends used to check on the old man sometimes. One time he told them he had been harassed. The Hermit
even named the culprits. She claims to have made a statement to

During the Civil War, Fort Fisher was vital in keeping the Wilmington port open for Confederate supplies and commissions. The fortification was comprised mainly of dirt and sand, used to withstand explosives. The Federals were certain they could win the war if they could secure Fort Fisher. On December 7, 1864, Union soldiers fired on the stronghold for twenty days but were deterred by Confederate troops. The Federals began their second assault on Fort Fisher on January 13, 1865. The Confederates put up a brave counter-attack but were forced to surrender two days later. Two thousand men died defending Fort Fisher. Unaccountable footsteps have been heard and a ghostly apparition of a Confederate officer has been seen looking over the rampart toward the sea. Some believe it is the ghost of General William Whiting, a fort commander who was wounded during battle and who later died in a prison camp.

Fort Fisher was expanded under the direction of Colonel William Lamb. Five hundred to a thousand free men, slaves, and Confederate soldiers were used to renovate the fort.

that effect to the local authorities after the Hermit's death, but Sheriff Grohman doesn't recall any such statement. Rumors of five rough locals harassing the Hermit on the night of his death remain unproven.

Some time after the mysterious video about the hermit was produced, authorities reopened the investigation into the death of Robert Edward Harrell. The SBI questioned a suspect but didn't have any proof against him, so no one was charged. The body was sent to Chapel Hill, where the state's chief coroner performed the autopsy. The medical examiner said there wasn't much of a body left so it was hard to tell. He seconded the earlier conclusion of "natural death."

The Hermit Society was founded in 1993 by Harrell's biggest fans to uncover the truth. Unfortunately, they were unable to put the mystery to rest. Did something sinister happen to the Hermit that night, or is it all much ado about an old man who suffered a heart attack? We'll probably never know since the police captain

Ten percent of Fort Fisher still exists and admission is free to the historic site and to the Fort Fisher Civil War Museum, which was recently renovated. It is closed on Mondays and most major holidays. The museum houses an audiovisual presentation and interpretive exhibits. Call (910) 458-5538 or visit www.ah.dcr.state.nc.us/sections/hs/fisher/fisher.htm.

and photographer dispatched do not agree on what they saw at the crime scene and both the coroner and chief deputy who worked on the original case have committed suicide. The evidence and investigation file have also disappeared. Furthermore, Fred Pickler will no longer discuss the matter.

The land was never developed. It has become part of a state park. A Fort Fisher Hermit marker reminds visitors that Robert Edward Harrell once called the land home. In 1989, the Hermit's remains were moved from a cemetery in Shelby, North Carolina, back to the Fort Fisher area. He was reburied in the Federal Point Methodist Church Cemetery. It is said that on the anniversary of his death, voices have been heard where he lived. Visitors to Fort Fisher can follow Hermit Trail, which leads to his beloved marshland.

The Mystery of the Brown Mountain Lights

Linville

Despite sightings by hundreds of residents and visitors alike over the years, as well as numerous official and unofficial investigations, the Brown Mountain Lights will remain one of life's little mysteries as well as the state's biggest and best-known legend.

In the foothills of the Blue Ridge Mountains, this small, 2,600-foot elevation in Burke County would rarely be discussed or visited if it weren't home to the mysterious lights. Just what the lights look like is as big a source of dispute as their origin. Some see a small reddish light that rises over the summit and then disappears shortly thereafter. It appears again within minutes but at another area of the mountain. It rises, hovers, and disappears. The pattern repeats itself throughout the night. Other witnesses claim the light is definitely white and moves in a circular fashion—appearing and disappearing in the same area. Still, others seem certain the light is like a glowing ball of yellowish fire.

I spoke to a young man from Thomasville who claimed to have seen the light and said it was a bright, yellowish red light that was round. As it got higher it got smaller and then disappeared. A minute or two later the same round, bright, yellowish red light appeared elsewhere over the mountain. It disappeared and appeared again further over on the mountain. This occurred several times.

My mother is another witness to the famed Brown Mountain Lights. She told me that her father once took the family to the mountains and they saw the notorious lights. She was very young at the time, around ten or eleven years old, and can't recall much about them. She thinks there were more than one and that the lights "flicked on and off" several times. Whether the light is white, red, or yellow—stationary or in motion—there is no argument among spectators that they saw vanishing lights whose origin was difficult to determine.

Residents of the mountain community say the lights started with the disappearance of a local woman in 1850. It was popularly believed that her husband killed her and hid the body. Locals participated in the hunt for the missing woman. While searching for her, participants noticed eerie lights shining over Brown Mountain. They had never seen anything like them before. Understandably, many were scared by the sudden appearance of the inexplicable lights. Despite search efforts, the woman's body was not found. Blood that was believed to be the missing woman's was found, but the husband said it belonged to a pig he had butchered. Since this was before the days of DNA tests, there was no way to prove whose blood it was.

Soon afterwards, a man who was new to the community and seemed to have little or no money was seen leaving town in a new wagon and horse that belonged to the missing woman's husband. The man said he had bought the horse and wagon. Believing he didn't have the money to have made such a purchase, locals concluded he had taken part in the murder and was given the horse and wagon as payment.

It was years before the remains of the body were discovered. The skeleton was identified as belonging to the missing woman. Many believe these lights are the lingering spirit of the dead woman. Some argue the lights were seen before the 1800s so they couldn't have anything to do with the murdered woman.

There is also a story about a pioneer family who built a home on Jonas Ridge. The father fought in the Revolutionary War and when he returned home, he found the house had been burned to the ground and his family was gone. The man searched caves and coves, using a torch at night. After many days without food or rest,

he collapsed and soon died on top of Brown Mountain. Many believe his spirit is still looking for his wife and children and that it is the source of the mysterious light.

Other theories include:

- Boyish pranks
- Divine power
- Hunters carrying lanterns
- Moonshiners "firing" their stills
- Spirits of Catawba and Cherokee warriors killed during battle
- Spirits of Catawba and Cherokee maidens searching for loved warriors who died in battle
- Spirit of a slave looking for his master, who was wounded while hunting.

Of course, scientists dismiss the folklore, although they haven't done much better in their efforts to solve the conundrum. Two investigations were made by the U.S. Geological Survey. The latter one was in 1922. A federal government geologist was sent to study the lights. The man brought tools, such as topographic maps, barometers, and telescopic equipment. He spent weeks investigating. At the end of his lengthy study, he deduced the lights were caused by many factors:

- 47% of the lights were caused by car headlights.
- 33% of the lights were caused by locomotive lights.
- 10% of the lights were caused by fixed lights.
- 10% of the lights were caused by brush fires.

These findings did not satisfy most Brown Mountain residents, since sightings originated before railroad service began and before the invention of automobiles! Also, lights have been seen when there were no brush fires.

Through the years, experts have also cited these theories:

- Deposits of minerals ores (some from which radium is formed). *Radium rays would be invisible. Even assuming the rays were discernible, they would be consistent. Geologists now state the mountain is comprised of cranberry granite, so this theory is completely invalid.*

- Will-o'-wisp (*ignis fatuus*). *Hard to believe since there are no bogs or marshes in area.*

- Phosphorus gas. *No swamps in the area.*

- Reflections from nearby towns, such as Hickory and Lenoir. *Lights were seen long before the advent of electricity!*

- Fox fire. *Light is not sustaining or bright enough for this theory to be true.*

Sign posted at one viewing area:
BROWN MOUNTAIN LIGHTS
THE LONG, EVEN-CRESTED MTN. IN THE DISTANCE IS BROWN MTN. FROM EARLY TIMES PEOPLE HAVE OBSERVED WEIRD, WAVERING LIGHTS RISE ABOVE THIS MTN. THEN DWINDLE AND FADE AWAY

Nearby points of interest: Mount Mitchell (at 6,684 feet of elevation, this is the highest mountain in the eastern United States); Grandfather Mountain (with its mile-high swinging bridge); and Linville Caverns and Falls.

- Andes Lights (a phenomenon that occurs in South America's Andes Mountains when electricity discharges pass through the clouds to the mountaintops, thereby emitting a light). This theory was brought forth by Dr. W.J. Humphries of the U.S. Weather Bureau. *This can only occur at extremely high altitudes, which would disqualify Brown Mountain.*
- St. Elmo's Fire (an electrical discharge that occurs in conjunction with a thunderstorm in certain atmospheric conditions). *The Smithsonian Institute dismissed this theory because this wouldn't occur mid-air as the Brown Mountain Lights do, and the lights appear without an accompanying storm.*
- Desert mirage (putting it simply, air currents of different and unequal densities could possibly produce reflecting surfaces from which really bright stars could be reflected). *Remotely possible.*

The scientific community is no longer concerned with the mystery of the Brown Mountain Lights, probably because they are unable to find a satisfactory scientific conclusion. Perhaps they have finally accepted it as a natural phenomenon or unsolved mystery.

There is even controversy as to the best place to see the lights. Some recommend taking NC 181 to Mile Marker #20, which is twelve miles northwest of Morganton. Others claim Grandfather Mountain and Blowing Rock are good spots. But most agree the best place is just off the Blue Ridge Parkway at Mile Marker #310, which is six miles north of Linville Falls at Wiseman's View. The best chance of seeing the lights is in the fall on a cool, clear night, and the best time of night is at 8 or 9, possibly even 10 P.M. Even if you don't see the lights, you're guaranteed a pretty view of the gorge.

Lydia, the Vanishing Lady

Jamestown

This must be one of the most widely circulated tales in the state. Many entries in the "Ghost Watch" contest were simply variations of this story. The original story is about a girl named Lydia who had been at a dance in Raleigh with her boyfriend. In the early 1900s, a road was paved that linked Greensboro to High Point. The road ran through Jamestown and a narrow underpass beneath the railroad tracks. The pair was probably discussing what a wonderful evening it had been, perhaps even making future plans, as they drove home to High Point. It was a dark night and drivers were not paying as much attention as they should. Lydia and her boyfriend collided with another car at the underpass, and Lydia was killed instantly. Ever since that tragic night in 1923, a young lady garbed in a white ball gown has often been spotted on the side of the road waving for help.

Burke Hardison is one of the motorists who have seen the specter. It was very late as he passed through Jamestown. As Hardison approached the underpass, he saw a girl wearing a light-colored dress. She was frantically signaling for help. Knowing something must be terribly wrong for this lovely young woman to

Vandals have spray-painted "Lydia is here" on the inside of the underpass where Lydia was killed.

be all dressed up and standing alone on the side of the road at that time of night, he quickly pulled over.

"What's the matter?" Hardison asked with concern. The girl told him that she was desperately trying to get home to High Point. "My mother will be terribly worried," she said softly. He told her to get in and he would gladly take her home. She said, "Thank you," and gave him the address as she got in the vehicle. Lydia leaned wearily back in the seat and offered no more information as she closed her eyes. Although he was dying of curiosity, Hardison didn't ask her any questions.

He knew how to get to the street she had named so he turned off the highway and continued without saying a word. He glanced over at his passenger and noticed she looked as if she was sleeping. Hardison wondered how long she had been waiting for someone to come by. What was her story? He thought he might find out when they reached their destination, but when he went around to open her door, she was gone. It wasn't possible, but she had vanished!

Determined to get to the bottom of the bizarre occurrence,

This is the original underpass where Lydia was killed. It is located about a hundred feet from the underpass now in use.

Hardison marched up to the door and knocked. After a few minutes, a woman answered. Before the odd tale could be told, the sad-looking woman said, "I know why you're here. You think you picked up my daughter. You're not the first person this has happened to, and you almost assuredly won't be the last." She explained how her daughter had been killed in a car wreck some years ago. The woman told him that motorists occasionally showed up claiming they had given a girl a ride home but she had disappeared upon arriving at the house.

She seems so tired and troubled that no one ever presses the girl for more information. The few times those who picked her up tried, all they got out of her was that her name was Lydia and that she wanted to get home as soon as possible. With tears welling up in her eyes, the woman told Hardison that she wished someone could bring her daughter home.

I interviewed a Jamestown resident who thinks he saw Lydia when he was a teenager. Years ago, there was a dirt road that extended to the area around the underpass. He was out one rainy night with some other youths on that road when his truck got stuck in the mud. The boys got out to push the vehicle and he saw something white behind him. They didn't stick around to get a better look. They ran off and didn't come back for the car until the next day. I talked to several other longtime residents of Jamestown, but no one knows just when Lydia was last seen. I was told the best chance of seeing her was on foggy or rainy nights.

Pranks have occurred due to the folklore surrounding Lydia. High school students have outfitted themselves in fancy white dresses and appeared as cars approached the underpass. But those who say they have picked up Lydia on the side of the road say it is no laughing matter. They are haunted by the image of a beautiful young woman trying to get home but never quite making it.

The Family That Didn't Exist

Cedar Mountain

The Uwharrie Mountains are in central North Carolina and line the Yadkin River. Until the mid-1700s, Indians and wildlife were the only inhabitants, but white settlers began arriving in great numbers. Since that time, the area has seen many changes. Battles have been fought over the land, including some between the Indians and settlers. Moonshiners have made their home in these mountains because the hillsides and valleys make good hiding spots from the law. Most of the residents are descendants of "mountain folk" and wouldn't live anywhere else on earth.

The Reeves family serves as a perfect example. They loved living at the base of Cedar Mountain, a little part of the Uwharries. There were six of them, including the parents, Jubal and Rebekah. They lived in a small cabin without much money. But their basic needs were met, the home was filled with love, and, all told, the family was happy and content—until the winter of the influenza epidemic. The disease took many of their friends and neighbors. The parents took all the precautions they could to ensure their little ones wouldn't catch the deadly strain of flu, but it happened anyway. One by one, all four children came down with it. As a result of caring for them, Rebekah took ill with the flu. The entire family was terribly ill and teetered between life and death. There was nothing the father could do but witness two of his offspring pass away. Eventually, all the children died, but Jubal was unaware of the other deaths because he had contracted the illness and was hovering between life and death.

Miraculously, Jubal Reeves recovered from the terrible illness that had wiped out his loved ones. It wasn't until he was nearly well that the sad fate of his family was revealed to him. The grown man wept like a child when he heard about the death of his wife and four children. The dead had to be buried immediately to avoid spreading the disease, so they had long been buried by the time he learned of their deaths. The poor man hadn't even been able to say good-bye and bury his loved ones, which made it all the harder to take.

Family friends came in and scrubbed the cabin and brought food but ultimately left Reeves alone to grieve. There wasn't anything else anyone could do. Only time would help heal him and allow him to get on with his life. But time didn't seem to help. In fact, as time went on, things only got worse. Neighbors who came to check on him reported seeing a woman's dress and children's clothes drying on the line. The local shopkeeper said Reeves had stopped in a couple of times and bought candy "for the children." One couple who stopped by to see how Jubal Reeves was doing and to bring him a pie found him finishing his supper. To their astonishment, he had set the table for six—as if his family were still alive! No one knew what to do. He seemed to be carrying on as if he still had a family. Nothing anyone said made the man react to the contrary.

Finally, the minister was sent to talk to the pitiful man. After spending hours counseling Jubal Reeves, he left feeling as if his parishioner hadn't heard a word he had said. Shortly thereafter, Jubal Reeves sold some land and gave the proceeds to the local shopkeeper so that the merchant would periodically deliver food and supplies. He was seen by passersby chopping wood and tending to other daily responsibilities, but he never left the area around his cabin. He became a recluse.

A traveler happened upon the Reeves homestead one night on his way through the mountains. As he approached the door to ask for hospitality, he heard the laughter and squeals of happy chil-

dren. The man decided to go on to the next place as he was hesitant to intrude on the family's merriment.

When he reached another cabin, a couple of miles due east, he eagerly knocked. The man of the house graciously welcomed him and asked his wife to give the weary traveler some supper. He thanked them and said he sure was glad they were so hospitable because it had been further between cabins than he had thought it would be. "What do you mean?" The traveler then explained how he had planned to stop at another cabin, but he had not wanted to intrude. The man and his wife looked at each other in puzzlement before turning their attention back to their guest. "There's no other cabin nearby but the Reeves place, and Jubal lives alone. Lost his wife and kids in a big epidemic we had in these parts some years back. Never got over it, poor man," he explained.

"That can't be!" the traveler sputtered as he dropped his spoon in disbelief. "I heard a man and a woman talking and then children laughing and carrying on. I know I did!"

Over the years, there were others who made the same claim—that they heard a family laughing and talking inside the cabin. Some say it was the spirits of Jubal's wife and children, back to help him cope with the physical loss of his loved ones.

When he passed away, Jubal Reeves was buried next to his wife and children. Their graves are deep in the forests of the Uwharrie Mountains. Old timers still remember the tale of the phantom family.

The Wrath of Old Squire

Benson/Four Oaks

In May 1820, a man known as Master Lynch took his slave, Old Squire, to the banks of Mill Creek to hoe cotton. The man stood over him like a tyrant, shouting at him to work harder or faster. Anger boiled up in the slave as he endured the berating comments and commands. Finally, he couldn't take anymore. In a fit of rage, Old Squire raised the hoe high up in the air, swung around, and brought it down on his master's head. Lynch screamed in pain as the tool hit him squarely on the side of his head. Instinctively, he raised his arms up to the wound but fell to the ground before his hands reached his head.

Old Squire carefully leaned down and inspected the crumpled body. There was no sign of life. He gently kicked the man's leg, but there was no response. After a quick check Old Squire realized the man was dead. He had killed Master Lynch. Nervously, he looked all around but realized no one had witnessed what had happened. He quickly dragged the corpse under the bridge and started digging. When he had dug a hole big enough to conceal the body, the slave threw down the tool and half-carried, half-rolled Lynch into the small pit. When the task was finished, Old Squire went back

to the creek bank and continued to hoe the cotton as if nothing had happened.

At the end of the day he returned to the plantation and had supper. Someone knocked on his door as he was retiring for the evening. It was Lynch's oldest son, inquiring as to the whereabouts of his father. "Sorry to bother you, Old Squire, but my father hasn't come home and we're asking everyone if they've seen him today. He left this morning and no one seems to know where he went." Trying to keep his heart from beating out of his chest, the slave slowly answered, "I think I seen him near the barn early this morning but not after."

Despite an extensive search, the body was never discovered. No one ever knew what happened that day and how the slave came to kill his master until Old Squire confessed as he was dying.

There have been reports of strange sounds, best described as "moaning," and strange incidents at the site ever since the murder. Whenever anyone tried to cross the bridge carrying a light, it went out—even when there was no wind or breeze in the air.

The Inexplicable
Vander Light

Vander

A switchman was smoking a cigarette on the train's platform in the town of Vander when he saw another train off in the distance coming straight at the standstill train. The man dropped his cigarette and quickly tried to change tracks to divert the approaching train. The engineer also saw the imminent peril and sounded the train's whistle, again and again. It was raining hard and that must have drowned out the warning whistle. By the time the conductor of the other train noticed there was another train on the same tracks, it was too late to stop. Miraculously, the switchman managed to avert the disaster by changing over the tracks just as the train reached them. But he was run over by the passing train and his head was chopped off when the body was pulled under the car.

Since the 1700s, a light that looks like a lantern is sometimes seen in this area. If you approach the light, it disappears. Then, it reappears behind you. Legend has it that it is the ghost of the headless switchman looking for his head.

According to *The Fayetteville Times* photographer Billy Fisher, who grew up in the area and saw the light many years ago, it is ". . . a ball of fire. It shoots out of the woods and then floats just over the tracks and then vanishes."

29

Just like the mysterious light that has been seen by many over the years at Maco Station, near Wilmington, numerous theories have been advanced. None have been fully proven or accepted. And, just like the Maco light, it has been studied by amateurs and scientists alike. The proposed cause of the light ranges from street lights or car lights in Stedman, a town four miles away, to phosphorous gas, commonly called swamp gas. "I don't know the conditions there, but it's certainly possible. There's probably a phosphorous compound, maybe phosphine, and it does react in the air and liberates heat and light. That does happen around marshes," said Halbert Carmichael, a chemistry professor at North Carolina State University, when he was interviewed by *The Fayetteville Times* about the Vander Light.

Will we ever solve the mystery as to what causes the strange light that has been seen near the railroad crossing on Old Vander Road? Probably not.

Eerie Happenings at the Old Salem Tavern

Winston-Salem

The man finally got the door of the tavern open and then collapsed on the floor, barely across the threshold. The crumpled figure was taken to a room upstairs while the doctor was summoned. When the physician arrived, he sadly announced that there was nothing he could do to save the man. He was too far gone, the doctor reported. The stranger was kept as comfortable as possible until he died a few hours later. The tavern keeper and doctor looked through the few possessions he had on him, hoping to determine his identity.

They didn't find one clue as to who the man was or where he came from and no one came looking for him. So the corpse was buried on September 6, 1831, in what is now called the Stranger's Graveyard. It's now believed that the man was Samuel McClary, a well-to-do merchant from Charleston who was traveling from Virginia back to South Carolina when he took ill.

In earlier days, taverns provided more than drinks and food. They also served as shelter for exhausted travelers. Since these were the days of horse and buggy, taverns also served as good spots to wait out inclement weather. Old Salem Tavern had an outstanding reputation

Salem Tavern still stands today.

as a worthy stop for travelers.

The servants began acting peculiar shortly after the unidentified man's death. When the keeper asked them what was wrong, the servants told him they had heard unexplainable sounds coming from the basement ever since the man had died in the tavern. The servants also complained of "cold spots" in the tavern that they had never felt before. A couple of them claimed to have been followed, although they didn't see anyone when they turned around. Despite the keeper's assurances that nothing was amiss, the servants adamantly believed the tavern was now haunted.

Something happened one night that convinced even the keeper that something was amiss at the old tavern. A servant girl ran into his office one evening and screamed that there was something in the attic. Unable to calm her, he finally promised to go have a look himself. Admittedly, the attic was rather dark and scary at night, he thought, as he looked around it. With all the recent talk by the staff about the place being haunted, it was no wonder the girl had imagined she saw or heard something. Just as he started

The tavern was church-owned and staffed mostly by slaves, except for a twelve-year period from 1791 until 1803. George Washington stayed at the tavern in 1791.

God's Acre was first used in 1771. Today, members are still buried in the Moravian graveyard, separated in groups according to choirs: married men and widowers, married women and widows, single men and boys, single women and girls.

back downstairs, a shadowy figure appeared in front of him. Before the keeper could decide what to do next, the specter spoke. He gave the startled man instructions: "Let my fiancée know of my death." He disclosed his identity as Samuel McClary and gave the address of the woman he was betrothed to in Charleston. Then he vanished as quickly as he had appeared.

The keeper did as he was instructed. He wrote the young lady about the death of Samuel McClary. Less than a month later, the woman arrived in Salem to oversee the reburial of McClary. He was moved to God's Acre and given a proper tombstone. She also claimed his belongings, which had been stored in the attic.

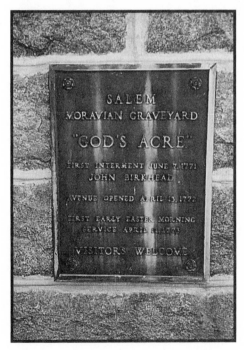

God's Acre Cemetery is on the northern side of Old Salem. Visitors are permitted to stroll through it.

From that day forward, there were no more strange sounds or sightings. There were no more "cold spots." Everything went back to normal. But no one forgot all the things that occurred before the man was identified, his loved ones notified of his death, and his remains given proper burial.

Lunch and dinner are still served most days of the week in the Tavern-Annex building, which was constructed in 1816. It is next door to the original tavern, which now serves as a museum. Visitors can explore the grounds of Old Salem and its shops for free or pay to take a guided tour that permits entrance to most buildings (including the tavern museum) and features a short audiovisual orientation.

This Living History Town is open year-round, except during Thanksgiving and Christmas. The Museum of Early Southern Decorative Arts is in the southern part of Old Salem and is free to the public. There is also a Children's Museum, which charges a nominal fee.

Thalian Hall Specter

Wilmington

Wilmington needed a theater and it had to be big enough to accommodate large crowds since the booming port city already boasted over six thousand residents. The facility also needed to be grand enough to attract celebrities and noteworthy acts. When it opened in 1858, everyone agreed Thalian Hall more than fulfilled its obligations. The theater was, and still is, an architectural marvel. Its style and splendor have been copied by other architects, including the man who designed the famous Ford Theater in Washington. Out of the thousands of actors who have performed at Thalian Hall, more than a few have claimed they felt an "unseen presence" backstage.

It's certainly possible, since the theater is reputedly haunted by two ghosts. They are believed to be the spirits of Maude Adams and James O'Neill. Both performed at the theater, although not in the same production. It's believed that Adams is the protector (or guardian angel) of Thalian Hall and O'Neill is the mischievous one, responsible for moving tools or playing with the stage lights. Once, a workman was above the main stage, fixing lights on the second grid. He laid a tool down. Later, when he reached for it, it

Thalian Hall as it appeared in 1909.
Courtesy of Wordwright Communications

was gone. It turned up on the next level, where no one had been and it couldn't have fallen without making a tremendous noise. The lights are dimmer lights, which means in addition to flipping on and off, they can also be turned from low to bright. On occasion, the lights have inexplicably gone from low to bright and from off to on.

The most intriguing experience occurred during a performance. One of the actresses had to make a quick change into an Edwardian costume that had dozens of tiny buttons that had to be fastened. In order to help the actress, the wardrobe manager always buttoned as many of them as possible while still leaving enough unfastened so the girl could put the dress on. Afterwards, the wardrobe manager carefully placed the outfit in her dressing room.

During a particularly hectic performance night, she realized she had forgotten to get the dress ready for the actress, who was about to finish her scene. Knowing the girl would dash offstage to change,

Thalian Hall is part of the League of Historic American Theatres, the Association of Performing Arts, and the North Carolina Presenters Consortium.

The theater is named after Thalia, the Greek muse of comedy and poetry. There is a portrait of Miss Adams on the third floor as Lady Robbie in *The Little Minister*. It's dated September 23, 1912. There is also a photo of Mr. O'Neill when he played the Count of Monte Cristo, taken January 2, 1902.

the wardrobe manager hurried to get the dress. But she couldn't find it. She ran to the dressing room to see if by any chance the costume was there and saw the dress as soon as she opened the door. Amazingly, the dress was partly buttoned—just the way she usually prepared the costume.

Thinking the actress must have taken the initiative, the busy woman dismissed the event and carried on with her duties that evening. After the performance, she discovered that the actress had not readied the dress for the costume change, nor had anyone else. No one associated with the production knew anything about it!

Stacy Edmunds, an administrative assistant at Thalian Hall, has also heard this story, but she doesn't believe a ghost was responsible for the costume incident because she doesn't think ghosts are interactive. Edmunds believes ghosts have left a powerful impression in space and time because they were such vibrant and energetic people when they were alive. Those intuitive to this can even see them. She's a believer because she has seen a ghost. It happened at Bessie's, a popular bar on Wilmington's historic Front Street that was formerly the Orton Hotel. Stacy was in the ladies' restroom when she was startled to see a black man, who appeared to be in his early twenties, wearing a string bow tie, enter the room. Before she could ask him what he was doing in the women's bathroom, he walked right past her through the wall! Edmunds figures he worked in the kitchen when the building was the Orton Hotel and the ladies room of Bessie's was the way to the kitchen.

Although Stacy Edmunds has never seen the ghosts of Thalian Hall, there have been sightings on the third floor of the theater. Those who have seen the ghosts describe O'Neill seated, wearing a dark suit. Adams is seen walking around in a black dress with a big bustle. Some patrons seated on the third floor of the theater have sworn they felt "cool pockets" or "cold spots."

In 1990, the performing arts hall underwent a major $5.5 million revitalization effort. Today, the lobby is where the back of the building was at one time. The entrance used to be on Princess Street, but it was moved to Chestnut Street when the 25,000-square-foot extension was completed. The new part also houses the box office, some offices, Studio Theatre, dressing rooms, and stage support rooms. Photographs of famous performers who have appeared at the theater hang in the new lobby.

Even though changes on the third level were minimal, mainly bringing it up to code, the ghosts haven't been seen since the renovations. Maybe there have been too many changes for Adams and O'Neill to continue to call it home, or maybe they are satisfied that Thalian Hall is being well cared for and they have moved on.

Or have they? A woman in a tour group a few weeks prior to my visit claimed to have felt a presence, according to a young man working in the box office. Miss Edmunds admits she sometimes experiences "creepy sensations on the third floor. There is a really old, antique couch and you will start to feel a little queasy if you stand in front of it long enough," the young woman explained.

Backstage tours of the historic theater are given weekdays by appointment only for a fee.

The Pink Lady at Grove Park Inn

Under orders from his doctor, Edwin W. Grove, founder and owner of Grove's Pharmacy and Paris Medical Company of St. Louis, Missouri, spent summers in Asheville in the late 1800s. His physician believed the mountain climate would be good therapy for Grove's chronic bronchitis. Not only did Grove's ailment improve, but he also fell in love with the area and decided to build a luxury hotel there. "The idea was to build a big home where every modern convenience could be found, but with all the old-fashioned qualities of genuineness with no sham. . . " wrote Fred L. Seely, E.W. Grove's son-in-law and co-developer.

The Grove Park Inn is certainly worthy of its standing on the National Register of Historic Places. Constructed in 1913, the impressive edifice has accommodated many famous people such as Harry Houdini, Richard Nixon, Thomas Edison, and F. Scott Fitzgerald. Many of these dignitaries and celebrities have shared thoughts that are now engraved in the stones that comprise the lobby.

Grove envisioned building one of the world's greatest resorts and there is no doubt the award-winning Grove Park Inn has achieved that purpose. Sitting majestically above Asheville, the

Grove Park Inn as it looks today.
Courtesy of the Grove Park Inn Resort

sprawling retreat was constructed with granite stones, some weighing as much as ten thousand pounds. The inside of it is just as grand as the exterior. The Grove Park Inn has ten floors, which hold over five hundred rooms and suites, as well as fifty thousand square feet of meeting space (including two ballrooms). The inn provides golf, tennis, two pools, an indoor sports center, shops and boutiques, a nightclub, and fine dining. Additionally, a forty-thousand-square-foot state-of-the-art spa was recently completed.

But what has drawn many guests and visitors for over a half century is the legend of The Pink Lady. It all started in the 1920s when a pretty young girl in a pink ball gown plummeted to her death. It has never been determined whether the tragedy occurred because she leaned over too far and lost her balance, or because she meant to take her life, or as a result of murder. Regardless of how she died, many swear her spirit is still present. Over the years, numerous guests and hotel staff have reported extraordinary experiences.

Many claim to have seen the figure in the pale pink dress. According to them, it vanishes just as quickly as it appears. Some witnesses say it is more like a thick, pinkish smoke that takes on the conceptual shape of a woman rather than a definitive wom-

The Great Hall of Grove Park Inn Resort
Courtesy of the Grove Park Inn Resort

anly figure. Others claim that what they see is unmistakably a female specter. Still others say they have sensed, rather than seen, the apparition. These witnesses say she has sat down on the bed next to them; they have sensed her spirit lagging just behind them when walking down a hallway, and they have even felt themselves being led by the arm.

The elevator is sometimes summoned to the fifth floor, the floor from which The Pink Lady fell, but no one is waiting when the elevator operator arrives. Lights turn on and off by themselves, as if turned on by an invisible hand. Empty guest rooms and bathrooms have been found locked from the inside, which is impossible to accomplish unless someone is inside. Keys do not unlock these rooms, so doors must be taken off the hinges in order to get them open. Even the hotel's typewriter has exhibited strange behavior. Used in the Convention Services department, the machine randomly types a few strokes or several muddled paragraphs. When it is taken in to be repaired, the servicemen can never find anything wrong with it.

Grove Park Inn Resort is located at 290 Macon Avenue, Asheville, NC 28807. Call (800) 438-0050 or (828) 252-5585, or visit www.groveparkinn.com. Other area attractions include:

- Biltmore Estate and Winery, boyhood home of author Thomas Wolfe (the house is currently closed for repairs due to a fire, but the nearby visitors center remains open).
- Cherokee Indian Reservation (featuring the outdoor summer drama "Unto These Hills").
- Chimney Rock Park; and the Great Smoky Mountains National Park (including the Great Smoky Mountains Railway).

Or opt for a self-guided walking tour of historic Asheville on a thirty-stop route known as "The Urban Trail." Popular activities for tourists and locals alike are hot-air ballooning and whitewater rafting. Asheville boasts many fine restaurants, galleries, museums, bed and breakfasts, and a couple of campgrounds. For more information, call the Asheville Chamber of Commerce Convention & Visitors Bureau at (800) 257-1300 or (828) 258-6101 or visit www.ashevillechamber.org

A painter who was employed by the hotel from the 1950s through the 1980s said that "back in the late fifties or early sixties, the hotel used to shut down during the winter months and that's when we caught up on painting. One cloudy, gloomy day back then, I was checking on some of my guys' work. As I got closer to room five forty-five, I got cold chills that got worse the closer I came to the door. It got so bad, I couldn't work up the courage to go in at all. In fact, to my last day at the hotel, I never did go back there; sent my boys in instead."

The engineering facilities manager also reported a strange sensation in 1995: "I was on my way to check a recent bathtub resurfacing in room five forty-five. As I approached the room, my hair suddenly lifted from my scalp and stood on end on my arms. Simultaneously, I felt a very uncomfortable, cold rush across my whole body. I didn't go in, haven't gone back, and don't ever intend to."

The painter had long since retired when the engineering manager was hired, so neither man knew about the other's experience. The strange encounters are not restricted to employees. Many guests have also had them, including the two-year-old son of a Florida college professor, the Kitty Hawk Chief of Police, and the President of the National Federation of Press Women. One might attribute some of these events to elaborate childish pranks or overactive imaginations, but these things have happened when there have only been a few guests staying at the inn, and they were all accounted for. Long-time employees are unlikely to make up such tales and have been the most adamant about not discussing peculiar incidences.

Hotel management used to discourage employees from talking about the ghost. They considered it bad for business. When, on the contrary, curiosity seekers began to flock to Grove Park in hopes of spotting the wispy figure, the inn began to embrace its legendary ghost. In 1995, management hired Joshua Warren to investigate The Pink Lady. Warren, an Asheville native and author of several books on the subject of The Pink Lady, spent the first six months of 1996 investigating the resort and interviewing nearly fifty people who claimed to have had unusual experiences or encounters with The Pink Lady. After his study of Grove Park Inn, he wrote *Haunted Asheville*, which documents his findings.

Just how does one determine whether a ghost is hanging around? For starters, Warren spent nights in various rooms at the inn. He was assisted, off and on, by three men. Mark-Ellis Bennett, who is a restoration artist at the inn, was in charge of conducting ultrasonic and subsonic audio recordings. Tim Vandenberghe, who is employed as a general technician at the resort, served as a field research assistant and was in charge of the infrared night vision scope. Tim Pedersen, Grove Park Inn general technician, also assisted in the investigation. Strong, unexplainable, electromagnetic energy was measured in many places within the inn. Two photographs revealed "ghostly mist" in a chair and in the background of an identification photo of Warren and Pedersen. One night Warren and Vandenberghe staked out Elaine's, the hotel nightclub. On that occasion, they used a Van de Graaff electrostatic generator. The machine measured significant electrical discharges. Vandenberghe also reported he saw a "white streak of illumination" while he was looking through the infrared night vision scope.

At the end of Joshua Warren's scientific examination of Grove Park Inn, he came to the conclusion that Room 545 is the most haunted locale in the hotel. It's believed that this is the room the mysterious woman was in when she fell to her death.

Media Relations Director Dave Thompsky told me that guests occupy Room 545 eight nights out of ten. Most leave saying they had some kind of Pink Lady experience. Thompsky is quick to point out that she is not harmful, merely forlorn or playful. When I interviewed him, he said that the last sighting occurred less than two months before our interview.

But who is The Pink Lady? Who is this girl who died so many years ago and still haunts the premises today? No one has any idea. Unfortunately, guest records are not available from that far back. Thompsky agreed that Warren's research was very thorough and that if he could not find the origin of The Pink Lady, probably no one ever will.

If you want to see The Pink Lady of Grove Park Inn, Joshua Warren's investigation indicates that the best chance is around midnight in the late fall and winter, and the best place is Room 545 or the main part of the inn. Even if you don't encounter the specter, just to see the legendary Grove Park resort will be worth your time.

Unstaged Productions at Aycock Auditorium

Greensboro

Located on the corner of Spring Garden and Tate Streets, the Aycock Auditorium was built to augment the University of North Carolina Greensboro campus. The college bought the land and tore down an old house that was on the property in order to accommodate the theater. The old dwelling was supposedly haunted by the spirit of a woman named Jane Aycock, who hanged herself in the attic.

Apparently, Jane has taken up residence in the school building. She has been spotted by the auditorium manager and by theater students. She is notorious for turning lights on and off in the auditorium. In fact, a switch on the lighting board is labeled "Jane's dimmer." Even though males and females have witnessed strange incidents credited to Jane Aycock, no female has ever seen the specter. Jane only reveals herself to those of the male persuasion.

Theater professor Tom Behm remains spooked by his encounter with Jane. In 1988, he was directing the musical *Bye, Bye Birdie* and had accidentally left his briefcase in the theater. It was late at night when he returned for it, so most of the lights were off. When Behm reached the middle of the auditorium, stage

Aycock Auditorium as it looks today.

lights came on. Next, the lights flashed on and off while a "... white kind of apparition, smokelike thing passed across the stage and came down the steps and was walking toward me." The professor admits he grabbed his briefcase and quickly exited the building. He says he has not been inside the theater alone since that night.

Theater major Jeff Neubauer and a friend locked up the theater one night in 1995. As they stood outside the building, the youths noticed a "very fair, white-looking woman with light-colored hair" walking past the window. Jeff figured it had to be Jane. There was no other logical explanation.

That same year, Aycock Auditorium Manager Lyman Collins met Jane. Having heard the stories, he was curious as to their validity. Collins picked October 31 to find out for himself whether Jane existed. He waited until everyone was gone and then headed for a spot Jane supposedly was fond of—the third balcony. Collins stayed a long time before giving up waiting for Jane. As he was locking the building, he heard the sound of piano keys. His heart thumping, Lyman raced into the auditorium and towards the piano. The noise stopped before he got near the piano, which had been previously moved from its usual place into the aisle while a

View of Aycock Auditorium as seen from the balcony.

painter finished working. The theater manager is sure it was Jane letting him know the piano didn't belong there. He now sees her as a helpful spirit, but many do not. While some say Jane is merely mischievous, others consider her downright unnerving or scary.

In September 1997, UNCG senior Michael Marlowe saw Jane. It was during the staging of the musical *Tommy*. He was in the basement when he saw "something in white walking up the stairway into the orchestra pit."

Neubauer had another encounter with Jane, and just like Marlowe, it took place in the basement of the building. Neubauer was leaning down, looking for a prop needed for the school's current production, *Phantom of the Opera*, when he felt a hand on his shoulder. The startled student raised himself up and swung around, but no one was there. Although Jeff Neubauer says he is not scared of the apparition, he refuses to go into the basement anymore.

The best chance of seeing Jane is to be in the building alone—especially in the basement, if you dare . . .

The Corpse in
Chambers Hall

Charlotte

Davidson College, located outside Charlotte in the township of
Davidson, was established in 1837. Fifty-six years later the North
Carolina Medical College was founded as part of Davidson
College, becoming the first chartered medical college in the state.
When Davidson College professor Dr. John Peter Monroe became
president of the medical school in 1896, he bought a small piece
of land from Davidson College and built a three-story building to
house the North Carolina Medical College. Cadavers were kept in
the basement and the anatomy lab was located on the top floor.
(Several years later the medical school moved to 6th and Church
Streets and the building became the Churchill Apartments Hotel.)

In those days, a Davidson student paid $75 a year in tuition and
an additional $80 for room and board. Reportedly, if students
could provide cadavers they were exempt from paying tuition. In
1889, there were only two students at the medical school, but by
1904 there were nearly eighty-five students. As enrollment
increased, so did the need for cadavers. An issue of *The
Davidsonian* from 1960 has a story about how Sam A. Thompson
confessed that he began exhuming corpses in 1899 when four
medical students boarded with his family for the school year. He

Main building of North Carolina Medical College, 1898.
Courtesy of Davidson College Library Archives

revealed that the snatched bodies were delivered to the school late at night. Thompson says he kept track of recent burials and joined students to exhume the bodies. A mule-drawn carriage was used to transport the corpses to the school. The grave robber recounted a close call they had one night. The small group were on their way back to campus with a freshly exhumed cadaver when they came upon some men on the side of the road. The men stared at the corpse, which was illuminated by the moonlight. The quick-thinking driver turned and shouted back "Come on and sit up now! You're not that drunk!" The ruse worked and they went on to deliver their grisly load.

The school has steadfastly denied any knowledge of these activities. However, the following letter, published in *The Charlotte*

Observer on Sunday, December 4, 1949, further supports that grave-robbing by medical students really happened. The letter was written by a former Davidson College student, Walter Dumas, to prominent Charlotte citizen Howard B. Arbuckle Jr. The article includes a photograph of Arbuckle holding a skull sent by Dumas. (Author's note: Grammar and punctuation are as the letter appeared in the newspaper.)

Dear Howard:

Through the courtesy of John Williams—"Shorty"—who is now in San Francisco with his work with the Extension Division of the University of Pennsylvania, I have been given your address. May I presume on our long though interrupted acquaintance and our mutual interest in Beta chapter of Pi Kappa Alpha to ask you to perform a small task for me?

Under a separate cover I am sending to you by parcel post a skull, which I shall appreciate your kindness in presenting with such suitable ceremony as may be indicated, to the chapter, in my name.

This is no ordinary skull. At the time I was a student at Davidson, there was a legend that somewhere about the turn of the century when Davidson had a Medical School, later moved, I believe, to Charlotte, and still later to Charlottesville, where it became the nucleus of the University of Virginia, the anatomy laboratory was in the building which in my day [was] the Biology laboratory and (strange coincidence) the College Infirmary.

According to the legend, the medical students, not having access to bodies otherwise destined for the Potter's Field, as is the case now, were required to furnish their own cadavers, which they did by watching for interments in the local cemetery and visiting it for their surreptitious purposes. On one occasion they converted to their own use the body of an old Negro man. This man was the beloved retainer of a well-known family of the "White Folks," who, finding that the grave had been robbed, set the local authorities in motion. The students got wind of the impending blow, with the result that as the Sheriff came in the front door of the laboratory with his deputies and a search warrant, the students went out the back, taking "Archibald" with them. They climbed to the attic of the old Chambers Building, made their way out into the superstructure of the portico, which was supported by the famous old column, and dropped their burden down one of the columns and added a quantity of lime to destroy the evidence.

So went the story when I was a student. It had never been verified so far as we knew. Curiosity got the better of Skinny Campbell (Ernest G., as I remember it) and me. Skinny, you may remember, was the son of Mrs. Campbell, a widow who operated a boarding house next door to Mrs. W.D. Vinson's, which was home to me for four years. We knew that there had been attempts to descend the inside of the columns but always unsuccessfully because schoolmates of the would-be adventurers had always poured buckets of water down on the explorers, or dropped burning newspapers, or otherwise succeeded in rendering the attempts abortive, all in the spirit of fun, of course.

Skinny and I, swearing each other to secrecy, decided to make a thorough search and in doing so avoid the pitfalls which had beset our predecessors of several years before. Consequently a Saturday afternoon was selected when there was some particularly interesting athletic event in progress on Sprunt Field and the campus was otherwise deserted. We took a heavy rope, flashlights, and newspapers to the top of the columns under the low roof and matched to see who would have the honor of making the first descent. Skinny won. Fearing "black damp," we dropped burning paper down a column to be sure there was an adequate oxygen supply (thereby contributing to its rapid exhaustion), secured the rope to the roof beams and dropped the end down a column where the telephone-post-like piling which was centered in the hollow shaft of the brown stone column had been burned out in the previous attempts, and Skinny went down. Result: nothing. I went down the next column and found the skull, which I am forwarding to you.

When the success of our venture became known, it naturally created a mild sensation on the campus, was written up as a lead story in The Davidsonian (this was the initial year of that publication), was made the theme of a story in Davidson Magazine, a literary periodical which may not now survive, and because of its oddity was the subject of a brief story carried by the Associated Press wires. I received many clippings from friends all over the country. A few days later Skinny went down another column and found the remains of the rest of the body, which had, allegedly, been covered with lime. The skull had shown no evidence of such treatment. He found one forearm and hand with the tendons partially intact. A later exploration of the other columns brought negative results.

That's the story, poorly told (and abominably typed).

The skull has never been cleaned up and is in the condition in which it was found except for smoke stains on the inner side of the cranium, the latter being the result of a practical joke on Alexander, the fine old Negro who took care of my room in Chambers and came in early each morning to build a fire in the fireplace so that we might have a warm room in which to dress. It was our custom to hang our clothing on a chair near the fireplace to reduce the shock of diving into cold clothes in our rush to make chapel on time. On the occasion in question Alex had laid the fire. He turned around to find seated in the chair beside him a figure with a grinning candle-lighted skull. We made our own fire for several weeks.

It was my long intention to send the skull to Beta chapter when my son could be emissary when he entered Davidson. The best-laid plans, etc., and my son chose to follow me into military profession, and was graduated from West Point in 1945. He is now on duty in Tokyo, where Mrs. Dumas and I plan to spend Christmas with him and our new daughter-in-law whom we have not yet had the pleasure of seeing. My own active service ended there, where while serving as a G-I for the occupation, in General MacArthur's headquarters, I was hit at my desk with a coronary occlusion and was eventually returned to an Army hospital in the States and retired.

Recent information on Beta chapter gained from their much appreciated "Altar and Skull" tells of the fire at the fraternity house in 1945 and the loss, among other things, of the box and its contents. That prompts me to send the skull now, with the hope that it may add something of old Davidson tradition to their new domain.

*I remember with the keenest of pleasure the years I lived in
your home (1913–1916) while I was taking my M.A. and
the splendid hospitality of your fine father and mother. You
and Adele were then so small that you may not remember it.
Nevertheless, it has caused me to retain a real interest in your
career and to be proud of your own war service as well as that
you are now performing in these days of uneasy peace.*

*Your performance of this duty for me will cause me to be
sincerely grateful, and to hope that I may be able some day to
reciprocate the courtesy.*

With best wishes, yours in the bonds of pike.

Walter A. Dumas

*You will note that the skull itself disproves the story of 'an
old Negro man.' We have for years called the skull 'Ichabod'
for obvious reasons.*

WAD

Through the years, many writers have penned their versions of
this as a ghost tale. Combining what I have heard and read, as well
as these documented facts, here is my rendition, from the per-
spective of a young Davidson student who learns the truth about
the skull from an old doctor who knows the story first-hand. The
doctor begins:

"It's a terrible secret I've kept all these years. Four of us were
involved, but I'm the only one still alive," the old doctor told the
young student. "To tell the truth, it's a relief to unburden myself," he
continued. "It all started our last year in medical school at Davidson
College. We had a rare night out to see a show in nearby Salisbury.
From the time we disembarked from the buggy, it was all we heard.

"Everyone was talking about the tragic death of a beautiful
young woman whose family was prominent in the community.
While we were sorry for the family, we didn't know the girl, so we
carried on with our revelry. We stopped for supper and drinks after
the show, so it was late when we finally started back to Charlotte.
The cemetery is on the outskirts of town and as we passed it, an idea
occurred to us. We never should have acted on it, but we did.

"You have to understand that in those days medical students were
responsible for obtaining their own cadavers. This was usually
accomplished by some polite and discreet grave-robbing. By this I

mean that students dug up a grave without anyone being the wiser, especially the family of the deceased. This seemed a good opportunity to acquire the corpse needed to complete the term. We'd had too much to drink and weren't thinking clearly. The four of us made a hasty decision to dig up the girl's body. We found some shovels in a shed at the edge of the cemetery and used them. I had to break open the latch on the casket but it finally swung open. There she was, all right. Quickly, we wrapped her in a blanket that was in the back of the wagon and then loaded her in the bed of the wagon. We threw the casket and dirt back into the hole and covered it up as fast as we could. After returning the tools to where we had found them, we beat a hasty retreat. No one would have been the wiser if a big rainstorm hadn't taken place early that next morning.

"The storm washed away the topsoil that hadn't been packed back as good as it should have been. The next day when the father and mother went to the cemetery to visit the gravesite, they found

> In parts of Europe, when a new cemetery was completed it was customary to bury a person alive in the first grave so that a ghostly guardian, *Ankou* (also called The Graveyard Watcher), was created. The idea was that this tormented soul would frighten off unwanted intruders and spirits so that the dead would not be disturbed. Wonder how they picked the victim?

a partially exposed casket. Unfortunately, they also found out that it had been broken open and that the corpse was missing. The father went mad! He swore vengeance on the graverobbers who had taken his daughter. A huge hunt was organized, led by the local sheriff.

"Meanwhile, we had arrived back at the college and brought the body to my room. Exhausted from the ordeal, we slept until a commotion woke us up. A fellow med student told us the authorities were at the dean's office demanding to search the school for the missing corpse. The father and authorities were sure med students had taken the body to be used as a cadaver. We knew this meant we would be arrested and subsequently expelled. A couple of us had planned to boil the body in a barrel that was used for that purpose, as soon as we could do it without arousing suspicion. This wouldn't be difficult because the school never asked too many questions as to where the cadavers came from. But now there was no time for that. We had to hide it, and fast.

"There was an entrance to the attic in the farthest corner of the floor our rooms were on. We took the bundle and a lantern and proceeded as quickly as we could down the hall. I climbed up on my buddy's shoulders and pulled on the small hook that was attached to the ceiling. It opened the door that held the stairs to the attic. I yanked as hard as I could, which unfolded them so fast the bottom steps nearly took off my head. We half-ran, half-stumbled up the stairs, awkwardly carrying the wrapped body. There wasn't anything up there. If we just left the body in the attic, it would have been easily discovered. Just as panic was really setting in, we saw that the top of one of the giant hollow columns had come loose. My roommate scrambled back down the tiny opening to get some tools.

"It seemed like forever before he returned. 'They're on their way to search our building next, I just heard!' he breathlessly reported. As if our lives depended on it, and I guess they did, we worked to finish loosening the board. When our efforts were rewarded, we struggled to lift her up over our heads and then dropped her into the opening. With lightning speed we sealed the opening and got out of there. Almost immediately after we finished and got back in our respective rooms, the dean, accompanied by the sheriff and a well-dressed man, knocked on the door. They looked everywhere, from the closet to under the bed. 'Sorry to bother you boys,' the sheriff said apologetically as the men exited our room and headed down the hall. When they finished searching all the rooms and still hadn't found anything, the sheriff asked the dean if there was an attic or basement. The dean slowly nodded. 'This building has a small overhead storage space, but it's never used, so I doubt . . .' The taller, expensively dressed gentleman spoke up. 'Search it, sheriff,' he ordered.

"My heart skipped a beat as I realized we had left the lantern in the attic. The dean led the way to the opening and pulled down the attic steps. Many of us had gathered to watch the activity. 'Get me a lantern,' the dean commanded one of the students. The boy ran to his room and soon returned with one that he handed over to the sheriff. He nodded at the young man and proceeded to climb the narrow steps as best he could. He possessed a large frame that made the task difficult. When the upper part of his body was through the opening, the sheriff held the lantern up high and cautiously swung it from left to right. The big man remained on the steps as he surveyed what the light illuminated. After a few minutes, he descended. 'Nothing there,' he reported.

"The dean was promising there was no way any of his students could have been involved in such a terrible deed. All the while, the well-groomed man was insisting someone from the school was behind the theft. The sheriff wordlessly followed the two men as they left the building and walked across the campus. We held our breaths until they departed."

The old man paused in his story-telling as he relit his pipe. He offered me a drink. I declined. I hoped he wouldn't have one either, since I was anxious for him to get on with the fascinating tale. He made himself a drink and took a long sip before settling back into his chair. He took another swallow before setting it down on the table next to him. The doc chuckled as he noticed my agitation. "You're wondering what happened to the body, aren't you?" he asked me. I nodded several times.

"We were afraid to try to remove the corpse for fear of getting caught. After a tense discussion or two on the subject, the four of us never talked about it again. Over the years, students and faculty alike have reported seeing her. I am sure she is the same woman that you have seen," he said as he waved his pipe in my direction.

I gasped in amazement. "How did you know that I've seen her?" I shouted.

"It was obvious by the way you reacted as I told the story, but I already knew. It's no accident that you're here. I asked the dean who was residing in my old room and he told me that it was you. That's why I invited you out this evening."

I thought I had been invited to meet with the doctor because he was getting ready to retire and I was about to graduate. I thought he was looking for an apprentice and was hopeful he was considering me. As I was mentally sorting all this out, the old man watched me intently. "How do you know it's the same girl?" I finally asked. This time he nodded several times and then walked across the room to a desk.

The doc pulled open the second drawer from the bottom and extracted an item I couldn't see. When he handed it to me, I saw it was an exquisite silver locket, suspended on a long silver chain. "This fell off her neck while we were hastily transporting the body and I shoved it in my pocket and forgot all about it for a while." With trembling fingers, I opened it and found a photo of an exquisite young woman. No doubt—it was her! It was the face that had haunted me during my entire academic tenure at the college.

I told him about when I had first seen her and how I felt when I realized she wasn't real. I also explained how my friends all thought I was crazy until she was seen by a couple of other students. "Finally, we were told about the legend, but all we were told is that the spirit of a lovely young lady shows herself to a few people. No one knows what brought her to the college. It has been driving me crazy. I'm grateful that you shared your story with me, sir."

"Well now, I don't believe in secrets between colleagues, do you?" the old doc asked with a sly smile.

Hanging at Helen's Bridge

Legend has it that in the early 1900s, a woman named Helen lived with her young daughter in a small house located near a bridge and a secluded estate on Asheville's Beaucatcher Mountain. The little girl used to slip off to the abandoned mansion to play. One afternoon while she was there, a fire occurred in the room the child was in and she died in the blaze. The death of her only child devastated Helen. Unable to bear the loss, the heartbroken woman hanged herself from the old bridge.

Through the years, sightings of Helen have been reported at the castle, bridge, and surrounding area. Locals say that you may spot the apparition if you park your car under this bridge and call out *"Helen, come forth!"* three times. If she touches the vehicle, a tiny, permanent mark will appear there.

There are stories that Helen also haunts the castle where her only child was killed. Known as Zealandia, the castle was built in 1889 by John Evans Brown. He came from Pennsylvania to Asheville in the mid-1800s for a visit and fell in love with the mountain community. Brown bought 168 acres on Beaucatcher Mountain, but his wandering spirit wasn't quite ready to settle

down. He went West during the Gold Rush but returned home empty-handed. Soon afterwards, he was off again, this time to New Zealand to try his hand at sheep farming. He met with much success in this endeavor and returned to Asheville a very rich man in 1884. He also brought back a wife, the adopted daughter of a wealthy merchant. Brown started construction on his dream home and when it was completed in 1889, he named it Zealandia, in honor of the time he had happily spent in New Zealand. The owner lived in the castle until his death, a mere six years later.

At that time, Zealandia was sold by his heirs to O.D. Revell, who soon sold it to Sir Philip S. Henry. Born in Australia, Henry was a diplomat and scholar who received many educational accolades. His wife, Violet Lewisohn Henry, died in the Windsor Hotel

This undated photograph shows the exterior of Zealandia
before it was torn down.
Courtesy of Ewart M. Ball Collection, Ramsey Library Special Collections,
University of North Carolina at Asheville

fire in New York City just before the couple was to move to
Asheville. The guests were all told to leave the premises because a
fire had broken out. Despite the tremendous risk, Mrs. Henry
went back into the hotel to get some valuable jewelry she'd left in
their room. The ceiling caved in and killed her.

Some believe Zealandia's ghost is Violet Henry, who kept watch
over her loved ones and, later, others who resided in Sir Henry's
estate. During the thirty years Sir Henry lived in the castle, he dou-
bled the size of the estate and built an English Tudor mansion and a
carriage bridge leading to it. He was an art lover and collector and
founded the Asheville Art Association and Museum in 1930. The
multi-level museum was open to the public with no admission cost.
It housed rare and priceless items, such as Renaissance paintings, gob-
lets used by the Incas during banquets, an original manuscript of the
Jewish Torah, axes used by the Crusaders, and Ming Dynasty vases.
Sadly, this wonderful facility was torn down years later to make way
for I-240.

Upon Sir Henry's death in 1933, his two daughters, Violet and
Lenore, inherited the estate. The sisters married two brothers who

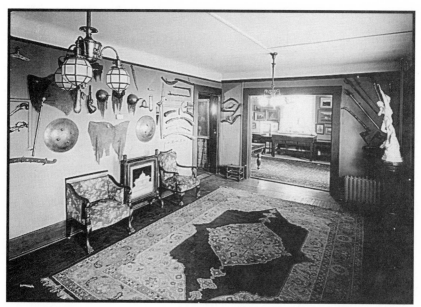

A rare look at the interior of the house during the time Sir Philip Henry
resided there. The house was filled with priceless antiques and art.
Courtesy of Ewart M. Ball Collection, Ramsey Library Special Collections,
University of North Carolina at Asheville

served in the British military. During the war, Zealandia was used
as an officer's club by the Air Force. Lenore's husband was killed
in the war and she sold her half of Zealandia to her sister. After the
war, Violet Henry Maconochie and her husband tried to sell the
castle because of the enormous tax burden, but no one was interested, so they had it torn down. The English Tudor mansion Sir
Henry built on his estate was left intact, and the Maconochies
lived there before they eventually sold it to the Dixons.

The Dixons used it as a spring retreat from their main residence
in Miami. Like Sir Philip Henry, they were art enthusiasts, but their
collection leaned more to furniture, including Marie Antoinette's
bed and the throne of Emperor Maximilian. As for Zealandia's
ghost, the Dixons and Henry's daughters all claim to have seen it,
even after the castle was torn down. Mrs. Dixon continued to live
on the estate after her husband's death in 1969. She remained convinced that the strange events were caused by the spirit of her late
husband, not by Helen or Violet.

Another version of the legend is that Helen was the mistress of

Some years ago, the Department of Transportation declared the aged bridge on Vance Gap Road unsafe and considered replacing it with a modern structure. The Asheville Historic Resources Commission and the Preservation Society, as well as some devoted individuals, played a significant role in saving and restoring the bridge.

one of the owners of the castle. She became pregnant and he refused to acknowledge that it was his baby. In fact, he wouldn't have anything more to do with her after she told him she was pregnant with his child. The story goes that Helen felt very alone and despondent and she hanged herself from the bridge.

The mansion is no longer the scene for grand parties with guest lists that included wealthy and influential citizens such as the Biltmores, who were entertained by top-notch performers such as George Gershwin. Through the years, the estate has dwindled from 168 acres to 16. The huge horse stables were destroyed by a fire in 1981, which is believed to have been caused by a vagrant who built a fire to keep warm. Since 1984, the sixty-two-room structure has housed the executive offices of Peppertree Resorts. But the legend remains. Employees still report hearing inexplicable noises such as beepers going off for no reason, feeling cold spots, and seeing file folders and mail fly out of drawers and mail slots.

Tragedy Aboard the Queen of Sounds

Outer Banks

Corporal Pierre Godette, or "Frenchy" to those who knew him, was stationed at Roanoke Island during the Civil War. The young man took to the area like a fish to water. When the war was over, he wrangled a government job on the island. Some years later, Godette was forced to find other means of employment when the government did away with the position. Fun-loving Frenchy had managed to save a fair sum, but it wasn't enough to support him for the rest of his life.

The reveler came up with a creative solution that would keep him gainfully employed without having to leave Roanoke Island. He used his savings to have a showboat built. Powered by a steam engine, the three-level vessel was made with the finest timber and imported furnishings. The main level held the ballroom and bar, which also contained gaming tables. The top deck had promenades and luxurious private rooms. Godette had spared no expense. He even had a player piano specially made for his gambling and party boat.

The vessel was christened the *Queen of Sounds*. The tunes the piano cranked out could be heard even by those on shore, which

drew many people to wave and watch as the showboat chugged by. The concept was well received. The *Queen of Sounds* made multiple day stops at Elizabeth City, Currituck, and Manteo. Performers were hired from as far away as Philadelphia to act in plays. The boat ran during the spring, summer, and fall. In the winter, necessary repairs were made. To most folks, Frenchy seemed to be on top of the world. He was doing what he loved and the boat was making him a great deal of money.

But Godette was drinking too much and it was clouding his judgment. He had always enjoyed whiskey, but now he was consuming much more than he used to. It could have been from boredom, but many believed it was the influence of his new girlfriend.

ar stratum of rock. This happens to be the same stratum of rock
that the house is built upon, which means that the vibrations carry
to the house. Since the door was measured and found not to be
completely level, the vibrations are significant enough to jar the
door open. The pressure of the intense vibrations causes the door
to open to relieve the pressure. This means that even if the door is
locked or blocked, the pressure causes it to burst open.

After this scientific-sounding explanation was dispensed, folks
felt better about the old house and the door, and the house was
inhabited again. The Jones family moved in and turned the run-
down house into a fine home. Late one night, some family members were gathered in the living room and the infamous door burst
open. But no train had passed through, nor was there anything else
that would have caused a vibration! This event contradicted the
rational theory that had been presented. Other former inhabitants
always claimed there was more to the door than reason. They say
secured objects have flown out of the little storage room and across
the living room and they have heard what sounds like shuffling feet
coming from the small room. All told, it is easy to understand why
no one dares to call The House of the Opening Door home.

She practiced black magic and got Frenchy heavily involved as
well. All the chants, invocations, sorcery, and related mumbo-
jumbo deeply confused him and brought out a dark side that he
had trouble coping with, so he drank all the more.

One summer night, he announced to some patrons that he was
going to conjure the Devil himself to come aboard his boat!
What's more, he proposed to do it Sunday night. This was considered blasphemy by all who heard his proclamation. Many begged
Godette not to go through with his plan. These were God-fearing
people and they knew no good could come of it, but there was no
talking the man out of the notion.

That Sunday night, the boat was closed to all but Frenchy
Godette and his crew. What happened aboard the vessel that night
will remain a mystery. Area residents said they heard the player
piano. Some claimed to have seen Godette standing on the top
deck. The ship's lights went out several times. Figures were seen
moving around on the decks, but witnesses couldn't determine
who or what they were. At midnight, a horrific scream was heard
just before the ship exploded. Those who saw it say there was a
flash of light (but not like lightning) and then *Queen of Sounds*
seemed to come out of the water intact but then burst into thousands of pieces. Afterwards, sulfur could be smelled as far as two
miles away.

There were no survivors to tell what happened that night.
Many theories have been brought forth. The most plausible is that
the boiler blew up. Some swear the Devil came and reclaimed
Frenchy Godette.

Legend has it that if you stand near the bridge that joins Nags
Head to Roanoke Island, you just might see the reflection of lights
on the water. It's believed they belong to the *Queen of Sounds*.

The Creepy Door

Hendersonville

In the western part of the state, on Salola Mountain near Hendersonville, there was a house with a door that became a legend. Off the kitchen was a small room once used as the servants' quarters, and later as a pantry and storage area. The door to that room wouldn't stay closed. For that reason, this house became known as The House of the Opening Door.

The railroad tracks were only about a mile away and freight trains made regular deliveries to Hendersonville, so every time a train came through, the shrill whistle of the engine could be heard inside the house. Every time the train roared through, the door burst open. It didn't matter that the door was blocked by furniture, latched, bolted, or nailed shut—it always flew open.

Anyone who ever lived in the house was eventually driven out by the bizarre phenomenon. John and Harriet Drew and their children were among the frightened inhabitants. They had never had much money and this was the first real home they owned. The family was excited about their new home and the future, until the first time they heard a train pass by. The train always roared through late at night so family members would lie awake

66

in bed waiting to hear the train and what always ca
Despite knowing it was coming, the sharp sound of th
whistle and the *chug-clank*, *chug-clank*, *chug-clank* that fo
the train slid across the steel tracks almost made them
of their skins. The loud creaking of the old door always
as it swung forward on its hinges. It was just too muc
night after night.

Eventually, the strange old house sat abandoned. Ma
believe the door would open, despite being locked or b
there wasn't some kind of scientific reason for why an
group of engineers, determined to explain the mystery of
stayed in the house for a few days. The men concluded
house is positioned on a hill of solid rock. Under the rock
places of dense soil, as well as spots with less soil than the
have. When the train goes by, its weight and speed jars a

67

She practiced black magic and got Frenchy heavily involved as well. All the chants, invocations, sorcery, and related mumbo-jumbo deeply confused him and brought out a dark side that he had trouble coping with, so he drank all the more.

One summer night, he announced to some patrons that he was going to conjure the Devil himself to come aboard his boat! What's more, he proposed to do it Sunday night. This was considered blasphemy by all who heard his proclamation. Many begged Godette not to go through with his plan. These were God-fearing people and they knew no good could come of it, but there was no talking the man out of the notion.

That Sunday night, the boat was closed to all but Frenchy Godette and his crew. What happened aboard the vessel that night will remain a mystery. Area residents said they heard the player piano. Some claimed to have seen Godette standing on the top deck. The ship's lights went out several times. Figures were seen moving around on the decks, but witnesses couldn't determine who or what they were. At midnight, a horrific scream was heard just before the ship exploded. Those who saw it say there was a flash of light (but not like lightning) and then *Queen of Sounds* seemed to come out of the water intact but then burst into thousands of pieces. Afterwards, sulfur could be smelled as far as two miles away.

There were no survivors to tell what happened that night. Many theories have been brought forth. The most plausible is that the boiler blew up. Some swear the Devil came and reclaimed Frenchy Godette.

Legend has it that if you stand near the bridge that joins Nags Head to Roanoke Island, you just might see the reflection of lights on the water. It's believed they belong to the *Queen of Sounds*.

The Creepy Door

Hendersonville

In the western part of the state, on Salola Mountain near Hendersonville, there was a house with a door that became a legend. Off the kitchen was a small room once used as the servants' quarters, and later as a pantry and storage area. The door to that room wouldn't stay closed. For that reason, this house became known as The House of the Opening Door.

The railroad tracks were only about a mile away and freight trains made regular deliveries to Hendersonville, so every time a train came through, the shrill whistle of the engine could be heard inside the house. Every time the train roared through, the door burst open. It didn't matter that the door was blocked by furniture, latched, bolted, or nailed shut—it always flew open.

Anyone who ever lived in the house was eventually driven out by the bizarre phenomenon. John and Harriet Drew and their children were among the frightened inhabitants. They had never had much money and this was the first real home they owned. The family was excited about their new home and the future, until the first time they heard a train pass by. The train always roared through late at night so family members would lie awake

in bed waiting to hear the train and what always came next. Despite knowing it was coming, the sharp sound of the engine's whistle and the *chug-clank, chug-clank, chug-clank* that followed as the train slid across the steel tracks almost made them jump out of their skins. The loud creaking of the old door always followed as it swung forward on its hinges. It was just too much to take night after night.

Eventually, the strange old house sat abandoned. Many didn't believe the door would open, despite being locked or blocked, if there wasn't some kind of scientific reason for why and how. A group of engineers, determined to explain the mystery of the door, stayed in the house for a few days. The men concluded that the house is positioned on a hill of solid rock. Under the rock there are places of dense soil, as well as spots with less soil than they should have. When the train goes by, its weight and speed jars a particular stratum of rock. This happens to be the same stratum of rock that the house is built upon, which means that the vibrations carry to the house. Since the door was measured and found not to be completely level, the vibrations are significant enough to jar the door open. The pressure of the intense vibrations causes the door to open to relieve the pressure. This means that even if the door is locked or blocked, the pressure causes it to burst open.

After this scientific-sounding explanation was dispensed, folks felt better about the old house and the door, and the house was inhabited again. The Jones family moved in and turned the run-down house into a fine home. Late one night, some family members were gathered in the living room and the infamous door burst open. But no train had passed through, nor was there anything else that would have caused a vibration! This event contradicted the rational theory that had been presented. Other former inhabitants always claimed there was more to the door than reason. They say secured objects have flown out of the little storage room and across the living room and they have heard what sounds like shuffling feet coming from the small room. All told, it is easy to understand why no one dares to call The House of the Opening Door home.